DISASTER ALERT!

Severe Storm and Blizzard Alert!

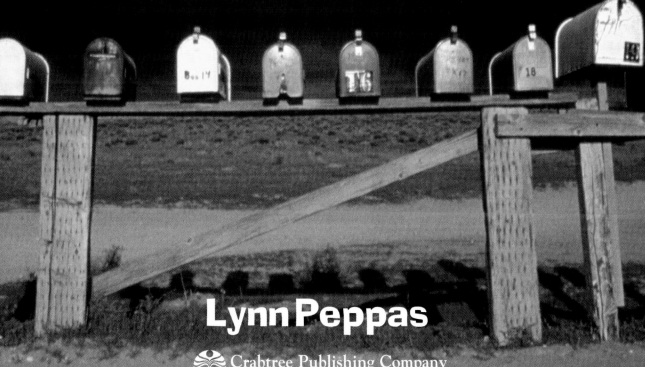

Lynn Peppas

Crabtree Publishing Company
www.crabtreebooks.com

presented by:

Crabtree Publishing Company

www.crabtreebooks.com

PMB 16A, 350 Fifth Avenue
Suite 3308
New York, NY 10118

612 Welland Avenue,
St. Catharines
Ontario, Canada
L2M 5V6

73 Lime Walk
Headington
Oxford 0X3 7AD
United Kingdom

In memory of my mother, Doreen Ellis MacIntyre, who taught me to love books

Coordinating editor: Ellen Rodger

Project and copy editors: Sean Charlebois, Carrie Gleason

Proofreader: Adrianna Morganelli

Designer and production coordinator: Rosie Gowsell

Art director: Rob MacGregor

Photo research: Allison Napier

Indexer: Wendy Scavuzzo

Prepress: Embassy Graphics

Printing: Worzalla Publishing Company

Consultant: Dr. Richard Cheel, Earth Sciences Department, Brock University

Photographs: AFP/CORBIS/MAGMA: p. 19 (top); Craig Aurness/CORBIS/MAGMA: p. 9 (bottom), p. 10 (top); James L. Amos: p. 15 (bottom); Bettmann/CORBIS/MAGMA: p. 3, p. 5, p. 16, p. 18 (top), p. 21 (bottom), p. 22 (left); Jonathan Blair/CORBIS/MAGMA: p. 28 (bottom); C. Clark/National Oceanic and Atmospheric Administration/Department of Commerce: p. 11 (left); CORBIS/MAGMA: p. 23 (bottom), p. 29 (bottom); CORBIS SYGMA/MAGMA: p. 24; Tim Davis/CORBIS/MAGMA: p. 17 (bottom), p. 28 (left); Digital Image ©1996 corbis; Original image courtesy of NASA/CORBIS/MAGMA: p. 12 (bottom); Weather Stock/Warren Faidley: p. 18 (bottom, right), p. 19 (bottom); Jim W. Grace/Photo Researchers Inc: p. 25 (middle); Aaron Horowitz/CORBIS/MAGMA: p. 11 (right); Dave Johnston/

Maxximages.com: p. 15 (top); Layne Kennedy/CORBIS/MAGMA: p. 18 (left); p. 21 (middle, right); Robert Laberge/CORBIS/MAGMA: p. 29 (top); David Lees/CORBIS/MAGMA: p. 21 (right), Lester Lefkowitz/CORBIS/MAGMA: p. 20; Sanjib Mukherjee/Reuters Newmedia Inc/CORBIS/MAGMA: p. 26; Viviane Moos/CORBIS/MAGMA: p. 14 (top); National Oceanic and Atmospheric Administration/Department of Commerce: p. 9 (top), p. 9 (middle), p. 23 (top); Northwind Picture Archives: p. 21 (middle left); Bryan F. Peterson/CORBIS/MAGMA: (title page); David Pollack/CORBIS/MAGMA: p. 27 (bottom), cover; Jim Reed/Photo Researchers: p. 11 (bottom), p. 12 (top), p. 27 (top); Reuters NewMedia Inc./CORBIS/MAGMA: p. 4, p. 14 (bottom), p. 22 (bottom); Galen Rowell/CORBIS/MAGMA: p. 17 (top); Royalty-Free/CORBIS/MAGMA: p. 9 (middle)

Illustrations: Dan Pressman: p. 6, p. 7 (top, bottom), p. 8, p. 10 (all); David Wysotski, Allure Illustrations: pp. 30-31

Cover: Wind-driven snow from a blizzard covers a stop sign.

Title page: Thunderstorm clouds darken a sky at midday.

Contents: Motorists who abandoned their cars during a blizzard, begin to dig them out a day after the storm.

Published by
Crabtree Publishing Company

Copyright © 2004

Cataloging-in-Publication Data

Peppas, Lynn.
  Severe storm & blizzard alert! / Lynn Peppas.
    p. cm. -- (Disaster alert!)
  Includes index.
  ISBN 0-7787-1573-6 (rlb) -- ISBN 0-7787-1605-8 (pbk)
  1. Blizzards--Juvenile literature. 2. Storms--Juvenile literature. I. Title: Severe storm and blizzard alert!. II. Title. III. Series.
  QC926.37.P47 2004
  551.55--dc22
                                    2004000838
                                    LC

Table of Contents

Force of Nature

Storms are nature's most common creations. At this very second, over 2,000 thunderstorms are happening around the world and 100 lightning bolts are striking the Earth. Rainstorms bring gentle precipitation but thunderstorms bring lightning, thunder, and strong winds. Blizzards release the same swift, bitter winds but happen in colder climates and bring snow.

Stormy weather confused ancient peoples. They believed spirits controlled lightning, thunder, and rain. These spirits, in the form of gods or animals, were thought to unleash the power of severe weather to do harm. The science of storms was yet to be discovered.

What is a disaster? A disaster is a destructive event that affects the natural world and human communities. Some disasters are predictable and others occur without warning. Coping successfully with a disaster depends on a community's preparation.

Commuters in India push a vehicle stranded in heavy rainwaters. The rain came after a dry spell, or drought, and caught people unprepared.

What is a storm?

Today, we know that stormy weather is not caused by angry spirits but by strong winds and clouds filled with precipitation. Knowing how and why storms form, and how to stay safe during them, makes storms less frightening. Storms and blizzards can be dangerous but they are also interesting to watch, and fascinating to study.

Storm myths

Thousands of years ago, people all around the world believed that gods who lived in the sky controlled the weather. The ancient Greeks believed that the King of the gods, Zeus, ruled over humans and weather and sent violent storms and lightning bolts to punish people for being bad. In northern Europe, the Norse called their god of thunderstorms Thor. They imagined that Thor carried a magical hammer that crashed down on the tops of thunderclouds and sent lightning bolts through the air. Some legends say that Thor's chariot made the noise of thunder as it rumbled through the sky.

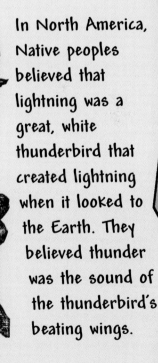

In North America, Native peoples believed that lightning was a great, white thunderbird that created lightning when it looked to the Earth. They believed thunder was the sound of the thunderbird's beating wings.

Thor, the Norse god of thunder.

Sun, Sky, and Wind

The atmosphere is a huge blanket of gases that is constantly moving more than 600 miles (965 kilometers) above the Earth's surface. The gases in the atmosphere make up the air we breathe. The atmosphere keeps the temperature from getting too hot at the equator, and too cold at the poles.

Protective layers

The layer of atmosphere closest to the Earth, where all weather occurs, is called the troposphere. The stratosphere, above the troposphere, has a layer of ozone that protects the surface of the Earth by screening out harmful **ultraviolet rays** from the sun. Without the ozone layer, all living things on Earth would be burned by the sun and die.

What makes weather?

The sun's energy is responsible for Earth's seasons and weather. Seasons and weather change because the sun heats the Earth's surface unevenly. The temperature around the **equator** is constantly warm. The temperatures around the polar regions are constantly very cold. Between the equator and polar regions, are warm **temperate** areas that experience four seasons.

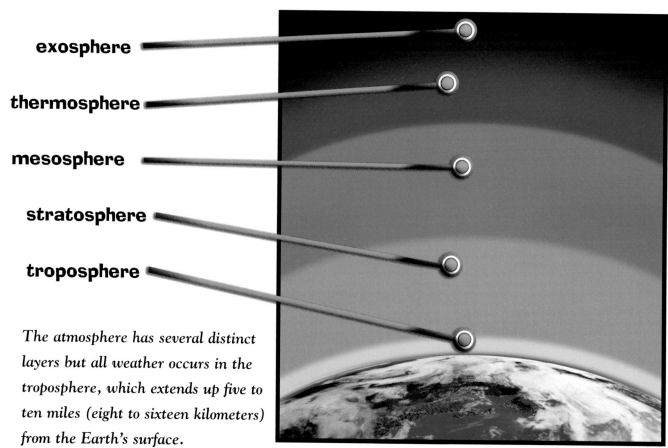

exosphere

thermosphere

mesosphere

stratosphere

troposphere

The atmosphere has several distinct layers but all weather occurs in the troposphere, which extends up five to ten miles (eight to sixteen kilometers) from the Earth's surface.

Wind and weather

Air masses also effect weather. Air is made of many **particles** that we cannot see. Air pressure, sometimes called barometric or atmospheric pressure, depends on how close particles are to each other in an air mass. Warm air rises above cool air because it is lighter. The rising is due to **convection**. When the sun heats air particles, the particles move faster and bounce off each other more frequently. Heated air masses also rise. A rising, warm air mass is called a low pressure mass. Low pressure usually means clouds and precipitation. Cool air is denser and heavier than warm air. Cool air sinks to the ground creating a high pressure air mass. High pressure air usually means clear and dry weather. Changes in air pressure create wind.

(above) Water vapor rises with warm air (red arrows) while cool air (blue arrows) replaces the warm air, creating wind. As water vapor cools it condenses into clouds and rain.

The Earth's axis at the North Pole

Tropic of Cancer

Equator

Tropic of Capricorn

South Pole

Tilted

The Earth moves around the sun at an angle, tilted on an axis. It takes one year for the Earth to orbit around the sun. The sun warms the Earth's atmosphere most at the equator, which is around the middle of the Earth, and least at the poles. The poles are imaginary points of axis around which the Earth rotates.

Storm Science

Much of Earth's weather is caused by water moving around the planet. Two-thirds of the Earth is covered by water, most of it in the oceans. The water cycle moves water from the oceans, into the air and over land until it falls and drains back to the oceans again.

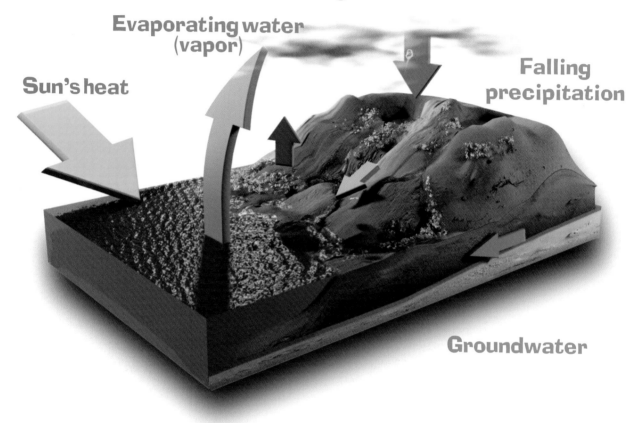

Evaporating water (vapor)

Sun's heat

Falling precipitation

Groundwater

Water vapor

When the sun heats water, it causes the particles in water to move faster, bounce off each other, and spread apart in a process called **evaporation**. Evaporation changes water from a liquid to a gas, or vapor. Water vapor is warm and light and rises through the atmosphere. As it rises, the temperature of the air cools the water particles. When the vapor cools to a certain temperature, called the **dew point**, it forms water droplets in a process called condensation. During condensation, water vapor changes back into a liquid. The liquid droplets attach themselves to dirt and dust particles in the air and form a cumulonimbus cloud, or a thundercloud. These clouds are carried across land by winds.

(above) Clouds traveling over land absorb water vapor from lakes and rivers. When a cloud gets too heavy and cannot hold any more water, precipitation falls to the Earth in the form of rain, snow, or ice pellets. Water is continually being recycled this way.

The thunderhead from a large cumulonimbus cloud. A thunderhead is the upper part of the cloud. Cumulonimbus clouds are heavy with precipitation and warn of a thunderstorm on the way.

Most cumulus clouds are thin and signal fair weather. When storm fronts move in, the clouds become heavy, taller, and move higher up into the atmosphere to become cumulonimbus clouds.

On the storm front

Meteorologists, or the scientists who study weather, call the meeting of air masses "fronts". There are two main types of air masses: polar and tropical. Tropical air masses contain warm air that moves toward the poles. Polar air masses are cooler and move toward the equator. At the edges of where the two air masses meet, stormy weather occurs. The term "front" came from meteorologists studying storms during **World War I**. They thought air masses fighting to occupy an area of the atmosphere was similar to armies fighting at a war front.

How Striking!

Lightning, a thunderstorm's most dangerous and mysterious force, is formed in a storm cloud. Lightning has the power to split trees, start fires, cause electrical failures, and kill people and animals. Thousands of people are killed by lightning each year.

Opposites attract

For lightning to strike, there must be two opposite and **electrically charged** areas. Electric charges begin in particles called atoms, which are so small we cannot see them without high-powered microscopes. Atoms are usually neutrally charged, which means they have one **electron** and one **proton** that cancel each other out. Electrons produce a negative electrical charge. Protons added to an atom produce a positive electrical charge.

What is lightning? Lightning is an electrical discharge from a cloud. Lightning usually happens during or before a storm.

The attraction between positive and negative charges builds until the charges trickle, then surge toward each other and create lightning.

Bouncing charges

Scientists are still not exactly sure how a thundercloud becomes electrically charged but they do have an idea why it happens. Lightning is thought to be formed when the **updrafts** and **downdrafts** working inside a thundercloud violently bounce rain droplets off each other. The process creates positively and negatively charged atoms.

Kinds of lightning

There are many different types of lightning. Forked lightning zigzags down from the sky. Ribbon lightning is several streaks of flashes that hit the ground. Sheet lightning travels from cloud to cloud. Ball lightning is a rare type of lightning that can be as small as a marble or as large as a basketball, and is said to float in the air until it explodes.

As fast as lightning!

To measure how far away lightning is, start counting, "one Mississippi, two Mississippi..." when the lightning flashes. Stop when you hear the sound of thunder. Divide the number of "Mississippis" by five. The answer tells you roughly how many miles away the lightning is.

Thunder is the "boom" heard after lightning. It is caused by the heating of the air surrounding a lightning flash.

Life of a Storm

Thunderstorms need warm, moist, fast rising air masses to form. The precipitation, lightning, and thunder of a storm are formed inside a fluffy cumulonimbus cloud. A thunderstorm can be as small as one storm cell but it usually contains many storm cells together, called a squall line. One storm cell can last up to twenty minutes.

Some massive storms, such as this hurricane can easily be seen from space.

When masses meet

Severe thunderstorms form when two air masses meet. The collision of air masses is called a front. Fronts are either warm or cold. When the fronts that meet are different in temperature and humidity, convection happens quickly, creating a tall, fluffy cumulonimbus cloud. This is the first stage, or cumulus stage, of a thunderstorm and it takes about fifteen minutes. Water particles form and travel up and down inside the cloud many times until they are too heavy for the updraft to carry them up again and it starts to rain.

Storm maturity

The first raindrop to fall from the cloud begins the mature stage of the thundercloud. The falling precipitation creates a strong downdraft of air that is much colder than the updraft. Warm updrafts of air still feed the cumulonimbus cloud during this stage, as heavy rain, strong winds, lightning, and thunder are at their peak. The raging weather usually lasts from ten to 30 minutes.

If the updraft is very strong, and the temperature inside the cloud is very cold, the water particles freeze and form ice pellets called hail. Hailstones can grow as big as softballs and ruin farmers' crops, dent cars, and break windows when they fall.

The third stage of a thunderstorm, called the dissipating stage, happens when updrafts no longer pump warm, moist air upward and the cloud begins to evaporate. The rains become lighter, and the winds weaker.

SUPERSTORMS

Tornadoes and hail occur at the end of the mature stage of a storm. One out of every 1,000 thunderstorms develops into a tornado, or "twister". They begin from supercell storms, which is another name for the most destructive type of severe thunderstorm. Supercell storms have wind gusts of over 58 miles per hour (93 km/h) and can produce tornadoes, heavy rain, and hail the size of golf balls. Tornadoes poke through the bottom of a thundercloud in a funnel-shaped cloud. Small, but fierce, with spinning winds of an average speed of 110 to 200 miles per hour (177 to 322 km/h) tornadoes usually only last for five to ten minutes. Hurricanes are the most destructive of storms and are called the greatest storms on Earth. Hurricanes occur over warm ocean waters near the equator. Hurricanes have winds greater than 74 miles per hour (119 km/h).

Life of a Blizzard

A blizzard is a severe winter storm with strong winds, cold temperatures, and blowing snow. Blizzards occur during the winter months in countries with cold climates and in the polar regions. With blowing snow and temperatures of 20°Fahrenheit (-7°Celsius) or lower, blizzards are dangerous, especially when people are not prepared to deal with them.

How do blizzards happen?

In North America, blizzards often form when a fast-flowing wind current in the troposphere, called the jet stream, plunges into warmer air. The jet stream usually separates cold polar air masses from tropical warm air. When the jet stream dips down, the warm air mass is pushed upward while the cold air mass sinks to the surface. The resulting storm brings precipitation in the form of snow and ice. Blizzards have gusty winds of 35 miles per hour (56 km/h) or greater. The blowing snow often reduces visibility to one-fourth of a mile (0.4 kilometers).

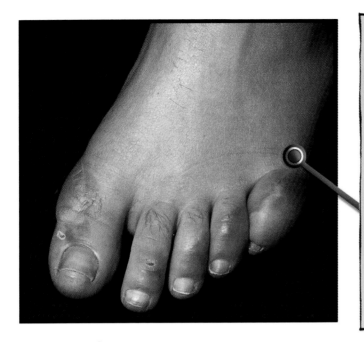

In extremely cold temperatures, the body protects itself by keeping blood flowing to vital organs, such as the heart and lungs. Less blood flows to other parts of the body such as the hands, feet, and ears, resulting in frostbite. **Frostbite** destroys skin tissue if untreated. Sometimes, the tissue must be **amputated**. Hypothermia is the lowering of the body's temperature. It is also a danger in severely cold weather. Symptoms of hypothermia include uncontrollable shivering and drowsiness.

Cccold!

In any blizzard, the combination of cold temperatures and fierce winds create wind chill, which makes it seem even colder. When it is windy, the air draws heat away from people and animals. A temperature of 30° Fahrenheit (-1° Celsius) outside with wind blowing at 35 miles per hour (56 km/h), feels closer to -4° Fahrenheit (-20° Celsius).

Blizzard watch

In some areas, blizzards occur more often because of prevailing winds. Prevailing winds are the most frequent winds in a region. In North America, a stormy, cold wind called a Nor'easter picks up precipitation over the Atlantic Ocean. Nor'easter blizzards occur anywhere from Newfoundland to Virginia. Lake effect snowstorms build over warm bodies of water such as large lakes and bays. Alberta Clippers are cold, polar air masses that bring winter storms east of the Rocky Mountains. When an Alberta Clipper reaches down as far as Texas, the storm system is called a Blue Norther. Buran winds, also called purga winds in Siberia and central Asia, bring fierce blizzards to southern Russia and central Asia. Poor visibility and cold temperatures make these blizzards very dangerous winter storms.

Famous Storms

Blizzard of '88

Natural disasters, such as storms and blizzards, can cause a lot of damage and take many lives. Some storms become famous because of their devastation. Each storm teaches us more about storm preparation and recovery.

The Blizzard of '88

People still talk about the Blizzard of '88 even though it took place more than 100 years ago, in 1888! What made it especially disastrous was that nobody knew it was coming. The storm hit the area along the eastern coast of the United States, from Maine to Maryland, on an unusually warm day in March of that year. Within hours the storm brought 40 to 50 inches (101 to 127 centimeters) of snow. Snowdrifts reached up to 40 feet (12 meters). Moving outside was impossible. The gusty weather brought life to a standstill. Over 400 people were killed by the storm before it moved out to sea.

(above) During the Blizzard of 1888, many people in eastern U.S. cities were taken to nearby police stations to wait out the storm.

Mount Everest

Mountain storm

At 29,028 feet (8,848 meters) Mount Everest is the highest mountain on Earth. Part of the Himalayan range, it is located between Nepal and China. Mountain climbers often attempt to climb Mount Everest and many lose their lives because of the extremely cold weather, unpredictable blizzards, and high altitudes. On May 10, 1996, nine climbers died after a fierce blizzard unexpectedly developed on the mountain, trapping them in the cold. Some died just short distances away from their camps.

Polar storms

The extremely cold temperatures at the polar regions combine with warmer winds to create the worst blizzards in the world. The fiercest blizzards happen in Antarctica, home of the South Pole. The windiest place on Earth is Cape Denison, Antarctica. Severe winds of 50 miles per hour (80 km/h) have earned it the name, "Home of the Blizzard." The Arctic has its share of blizzards as well. On May 16, 1995, the city of Tromso, Norway, located 200 miles (322 kilometers) into the Arctic circle, was hit by a storm with winds of over 100 miles per hour (161 km/h). These winds were so strong that they smashed through buildings and drove the snow inside.

Blizzard winds are so severe in Antarctica that it is dangerous to walk outside during a storm.

Mount Huascaran, Peru 1962

Storm avalanche!

Storms can contribute to other disasters, such as avalanches. In Peru on January 9, 1962, a winter storm dropped snow on an already heavily snow-covered Mount Huascaran. The next day the weight of the snow brought the mountain's ice cap crashing down. As the ice fell it collected rocks and snow from the mountain and by the time it reached the villages at the bottom of the mountain it was heavy and deadly. The 50-foot (15-meter) avalanche traveled 80 miles per hour (129 km/h) and crushed more than 4,000 people.

Survivors of the Mount Huascaran avalanche lost loved ones, homes, and livestock.

In North America "Hail Alley" is a north-south band from the province of Alberta to the state of Texas. One hailstorm can flatten a crop in minutes. Hailstorms can also be deadly. In northern India in 1888, hail killed 246 people. In Bangladesh in 1986, a storm dropped hailstones weighing over two pounds (one kilogram), killing 92 people.

Teguciga, Honduras 1998

A young man uses a log to cross a swollen river in Honduras. The river swelled after heavy rains caused by Hurricane Mitch. The 1998 hurricane killed 885 people in Central America and Mexico. It also left thousands without homes or jobs.

Storm of the century

Some people say it was the worst storm of the 1900s. It was so terrible that it is called the Storm of the Century. In March 1993, the storm began as a Nor'easter that hit the eastern half of the United States and stretched from Mexico to Canada. In Florida, thunderstorms brought 3,000 flashes of lightning an hour and caused many tornadoes. North of Florida, the storm turned into a blizzard with high winds and blowing snow. Altogether, the Storm of the Century killed 270 people. Some were killed by tornadoes, others froze to death.

The Storm of the Century lasted three days and cost an estimated three to six billion dollars in damages.

Weather Alert!

Looking as far into the sky as you can, you could predict the weather for only the next half-hour. To predict the weather for later in the day, or the next day, or the next week, meteorologists gather information about weather patterns that are occurring all across the world.

Before telephones and computers, people used the telegraph to send messages long distances. In 1835, Samuel Morse invented the telegraph. It changed the way weather was reported and saved many lives.

Weather forecasting

In 1868 in Cincinnati, Cleveland Abbe began publishing his weather "probabilities", which were weather predictions for the area around the Great Lakes. Terrible storms on the lakes were sinking ships. Abbe's predictions helped alert sailors to upcoming storms. Within two years, the United States Congress took notice of Abbe's predictions, hired him, and formed a nationwide storm warning network. What started with 24 weather stations in 1870, grew to 284 stations by 1878. All of the stations reported weather information by telegraph to the Washington, D.C. office headquarters at 8 a.m. and 8 p.m. each day. They supplied information on barometric pressure, air temperature, wind direction and **velocity**, **humidity**, and precipitation. The forecasts were not always accurate. Early forecasters did not have the knowledge of weather systems that they do today.

Scientists have been watching the weather and trying to measure it for hundreds of years. In 1593, Italian scientist Galileo Galilei (left) made the first thermometer. In 1643, Italian mathematician Evangelista Torricelli (right) invented the barometer to help measure weather conditions.

Ben Franklin's experiment

Benjamin Franklin conducted one of the most well known and dangerous weather experiments. In 1752, in Philadelphia, Pennsylvania, Franklin flew a homemade kite with a metal key attached to it during a thunderstorm. He wanted to prove that lightning was a form of electricity. Franklin was not electrocuted because the charge from the electricity ran down a wire he had attached to the ground. Three years later, Franklin invented lightning rods as a way to protect objects from electrical strikes.

Ben Franklin's experiment led him to invent lightning rods to protect buildings.

Sound and Satellites

Long-range forecasts give a general idea of what the weather will be like in a year by calculating the average temperature and precipitation of past weather records. Long-range predictions are not as accurate as short- or medium-range forecasts where information is based on current weather conditions from around the world.

Sharing information

Meteorologists get weather information from the World Meteorological Organization (WMO). The WMO gathers over 20,000 weather observations worldwide from land, sea, and air. The WMO is based in Geneva, Switzerland, and there are 170 national weather offices around the world. To measure the weather, meteorologists use different tools to help them record and transmit weather conditions.

Weather balloons

Weather stations send weather balloons up twice a day to measure and record the weather. Weather balloons, or radiosondes, are filled with **helium** or **hydrogen** to make them float. Radiosondes carry instruments to measure temperature, humidity, and air pressure. Around 1,000 radiosondes are launched twice a day at the same time all around the world.

This 175 foot (53 meter) meteorological balloon was launched from an Air Force base in the 1950s to study wind patterns and air turbulence used in long range forecasting.

Short-range forecasts predict the weather for the next two days and are correct about 87 percent of the time. Medium-range forecasts give information about the temperature and precipitation for the next three to five days. They are less accurate than short-range forecasts. Meteorologists' predictions are close but will never be perfect.

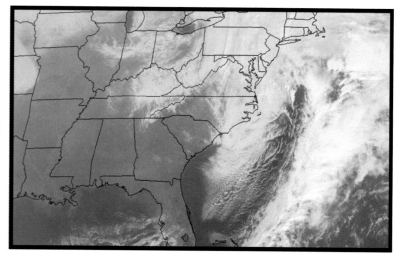

Doppler radar

Doppler radar provides important information on precipitation, wind speed, and wind direction for forecasters. Austrian scientist Christian Doppler discovered the Doppler effect in 1842. Doppler found that **sound waves** coming from a moving object change as the object gets closer to, or farther away from, the listener. For example, if an ambulance is coming toward you, the pitch of its whistle is higher than when it is moving away from you. This is because the sound waves bunch up as they approach, but spread out as they move away. The antenna from the radar sends out radio waves that are reflected back to the antenna when they hit a moving source such as wind or rain. Doppler radar, because it can map out air movements, is especially important for detecting tornadoes or other severe storms.

Doppler radar has improved the accuracy of weather forecasting.

Space images

Weather satellites take photos from space of clouds and weather systems. They also measure the air temperature at various levels, from cloud tops to land and oceans. Satellites measure humidity and wind speeds and relay information from one ground station to another. Data is collected by the satellites and transmitted every fifteen minutes to weather stations around the world.

All the information gathered from weather stations, doppler, radiosondes, and satellites is fed into a powerful computer in Maryland, U.S.A. The computer can make six billion calculations in one second – the same amount would take one mathematician over 420 years to do!

Storm Safety

The old saying, "Lightning never strikes twice," is not true. It can strike two times, or 1000 times in exactly the same spot. Lightning also strikes when it is not raining. Lightning starts about 10,000 forest and building fires every year.

Know where to go

Running for shelter under a tree is one of the most dangerous things to do during a thunderstorm. If you are caught in a storm, crouch down or run on the balls of your feet to lessen contact with the ground. Do not stand under trees. Stay clear of any tall towers, telephone poles, power lines, or fences. Metal objects attract lightning, making it unsafe to hold golf clubs, bicycles, or fishing rods. If you cannot get inside a building, a car is the safest place to be if you are caught outside in a storm. Stay well inside of the car and do not touch any of the metal parts such as the doorframe. Do not stand near large bodies of water while outside during a storm. Water attracts lightning too!

(above) A scientist tests the wind speed of a hurricane on a Florida beach. It is safer to stay inside during a storm.

Dangers around us

It is safer to be inside a house or apartment during a thunderstorm, but there are a few good general rules to follow.

- Avoid touching electrical wires, plumbing, and telephone wires.
- Turn off the television and computer and listen to weather reports on a battery-operated television or radio.
- Avoid showers during thunderstorms. Plumbing pipes can carry electricity.
- Have a flashlight and extra batteries on hand in case of a power outage.

Be alert!

Lightning is not the only threatening part of thunderstorms. Downbursts are extremely strong cold winds from the outer edges of a thunderstorm that travel down until they hit the ground. A small, intense downburst, called a microburst, can travel up to 170 miles per hour (273 km/h) and last as long as ten minutes. A microburst is especially hazardous to airplanes that are taking off or landing and is the second leading cause of airplane crashes.

Downbursts and microbursts are as dangerous as lightning.

Dress properly

The extreme cold and whiteouts of a blizzard are very dangerous. During a blizzard, the best thing to do is stay inside your home. Whiteouts strand motorists and cause accidents. It is easy to get lost outside during a whiteout because the ground and the sky both look white. Extremely cold temperatures and windchill can quickly cause frostbite and hypothermia in people who are outside for long periods of time improperly dressed.

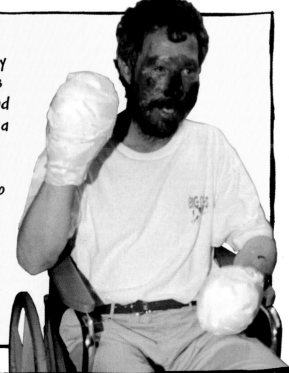

The blackened cheeks and nose of this man are the result of tissue damage from severe frostbite.

After the Storm

Many communities are equipped to deal with normal storms. When storms become natural disasters and the damage is too great for the community to deal with, they turn to government emergency management agencies and organizations such as the Red Cross for help.

Lending a hand

Government agencies help with search and rescue missions, clearing transportation routes, restoring power and communication lines, and distributing food, water, and emergency electricity generators.

Storm floods

Storms can lead to flooding if the rainwater cannot be absorbed by the ground. In cities, underground pipes called storm sewers carry water to lakes, rivers, or holding tanks. If there is too much water it will travel back up through sewer pipes and flood basements and streets. This water often contains sewage that contaminates drinking water and causes health problems.

(below) Flooding strands people in their homes without clean drinking water. Storm floods are often sudden and are very dangerous. During this flood in Jagatsingpur, a district in eastern India, soldiers in boats had to rescue people who were stranded on the roofs of their homes and atop farm buildings.

This is a test!

The United States Federal Communication Commission has designed an Emergency Alert System that notifies people in case of an emergency in their area. It replaced the Emergency Broadcast System in 1996. Information is posted on radio, television, and other sources to make sure that as many people as possible are warned of emergencies such as a war, or natural disasters such as a coming storm.

Ice storms damage power and telephone lines. Sometimes people are without power for weeks.

After a blizzard

Deep snow and snowdrifts bring travel in a city to a standstill. Emergency vehicles cannot get around to help people in need. If snowmobiles are available, they bring supplies and move people to safer areas. To clear roadways, snowplows are usually out during, and after, a blizzard. They push large shovels in front that scoop the snow before piling it to the side of the road. Some snowplows also spread salt or sand to melt the snow on the road and provide traction for tires on motor vehicles.

Blizzards make traveling hazardous. Even walking can be difficult, as the drifts cover sidewalks and curbs in cities.

Living Through It

Thousands of years ago, people believed they could chase away thunderstorms by shooting arrows into clouds. Centuries ago in Europe, people rang church bells, believing the sound fended off the worst of a storm. None of these methods affected the storms.

Animals have often helped people survive storms or blizzards. A thousand years ago, a monk named Saint Bernard ran an inn in the Alps of Switzerland. After winter storms, the monks took large dogs, now called Saint Bernards, to search the mountains for travelers who were too cold to go on, or trapped in snow from avalanches. Over the centuries, Saint Bernard dogs have helped save thousands of people caught in winter storms. Today, German Shepherds are often used in avalanche search and rescues.

Everybody's best friend

In the past, the Inuit peoples of northern Canada and Greenland used Husky dogs to help them travel in the Arctic. If caught in a blizzard, the Inuit huddled together with a dog team for warmth while waiting out the storm. Dog teams are rarely used today for hunting or traveling in the north. They have been replaced with snowmobiles.

Watching nature and the behavior of animals is a good way to see weather changes. Migrating birds fly in formation before heading south in fall. Frogs have sensitive skin and croak loudly before a storm.

Montreal has an underground network of walkways that makes coping with blizzards easier.

Escaping the weather

The Canadian city of Montreal, Quebec has more blizzards than any other city of its size. The people of Montreal have a fourteen mile (22 kilometer) network of underground walkways and shopping malls so that frequent blizzard conditions do not interrupt their way of life. The network is even connected to the subway so that people can move around without having to battle the cold winds and snow.

Snow in January?

Almanacs are books that offer regional weather predictions for the year ahead, among other things such as astronomy and folklore. The first popular almanac produced in the United States was the Old Farmer's Almanac. First published in 1792, it is still widely-read today. The almanac has a secret formula for determining long-range weather predictions eighteen months in advance based on the cycles of the sun and the moon and other "secret" observations. The secret formula is locked away in the almanac office in Dublin, New Hampshire. Although the almanac boasts of being "80 percent accurate," it also warns that it cannot predict the weather with total accuracy.

Recipe for Disaster

Try this storm experiment to understand how lightning is created.

What you need:

* Styrofoam plate
* Aluminum pie plate
* A flat-top thumbtack
* Pencil with a new eraser
* Piece of 100% wool material

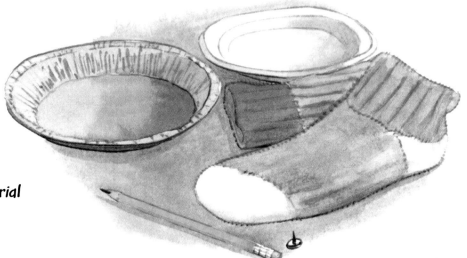

What to do:

1. Place the thumbtack through the mid-point of the aluminum pie plate. Make sure the head of the thumbtack is on the bottom of the plate. On the inside of the pie plate, put the sharp end of the tack through the pencil eraser. This will act as a handle for the aluminum plate.

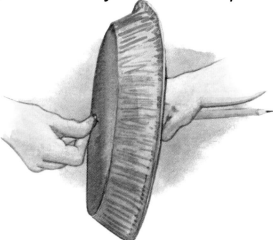

2. Rub the bottom of the aluminum pie plate with the wool material. Rub fast and hard for at least one minute. Get a friend to help if your arm gets tired.

3. Place the styrofoam plate upside down on a table top. Pick up your aluminum pie plate by the pencil (don't let your hand touch the pie plate) and place it on top of the upside-down styrofoam plate.

4. Now touch the aluminum pie plate with your finger. What do you feel? Try this again, but this time turn out all the lights. What do you see?

What you will see:

Lightning works the same way that these charged plates do. When you rub the plate with the wool material you are building up a negative charge on the plate. The aluminum pie plate, which is a good conductor because it is metal, allows the charge to travel from the styrofoam plate to your positively charged finger when you touch the aluminum pie plate. The spark you feel is like a mini lightning bolt.

31

Glossary

air mass The volume of air covering thousands of square miles or kilometers that is the same in temperature and humidity

amputated When a body part is cut off

convection The upward movement of heated air

dew point The temperature when air can no longer hold water in its vapor state

downdraft The sudden descent or falling of cold air to the ground during a thunderstorm

electrically charged Powered by electricity in the air

electron A tiny particle with a negative charge

evaporation The process by which water is heated and changes from a liquid to a gas or water vapor

equator An imaginary line around the center of the Earth that is equal distance from the North and South poles

frostbite Freezing of the flesh

helium A lighter than air gas that will not burn

humidity The amount of water in the air

hurricane A severe storm with very high winds

hydrogen A light gas that burns well

particles Very small pieces

precipitaion Water falling from the sky in the form of rain, hail, or snow

proton The positive charge of an atom

sound waves Vibrating waves that travel through the air

storm cell A low pressure disturbance

temperate A climate with distinct winter and summer seasons

updrafts Air currents that move upward, often followed by thunderstorms

ultraviolet rays Invisible light rays

velocity Rate of motion or speed

World War I An international war that lasted from 1914 to 1918

Index

 1 2 3 4 5 6 7 8 9 0 Printed in the U.S.A. 3 2 1 0 9 8 7 6 5 4